mud splatter noted 1/17 KK

11.90

THE SEASONS

Winter

Ralph Whitlock

The Bookwright Press
New York · 1987

Titles in this series

Spring
Summer
Autumn
Winter

First published in the
United States in 1987 by
The Bookwright Press
387 Park Avenue South
New York, NY 10016

First published in 1987 by
Wayland (Publishers) Ltd
61 Western Road, Hove
East Sussex BN3 1JD, England

ISBN 0–531–18141–3
Library of Congress Card Catalog Number: 86–73006

Typeset by DP Press Ltd, Sevenoaks
Printed by Casterman S.A, Belgium.

Contents

What is winter?   4

Why seasons happen   6

Winter weather   8

Winter around the world   10

How animals escape winter   12

How animals adapt to winter   14

Flowers and trees in winter   16

Winter on the farm – crops   18

Winter on the farm – animals   20

Christian and Pre-Christian winter festivals   22

Jewish, Sikh and Buddhist winter festivals   24

More winter festivals   26

Winter sports   28

Winter recreations   30

Winter clothes   32

Winter in art   34

Winter in literature   36

Things to do – Looking at nature in winter   38

Things to do – Making winter decorations   40

Things to do – Winter recipes   42

Glossary   44

Further reading   45

Index   46

What is winter?

What comes into your mind when you think of winter? Ice and snow? Long, dark evenings? Warm clothes? All these belong to winter, but probably the most important feature is frost. When the temperature falls to 0°C (32°F), water freezes. As nearly all things consist of at least 70 percent water, during a frost most life comes to a standstill. The exceptions are warm-blooded animals, including ourselves, who can move around and shelter from the bitter cold.

Some regions of the earth have no winter. They are in the tropical zone, which lies between the Tropic of Cancer and the Tropic of Capricorn. Most people who have lived all their lives in the tropics have never seen ice and snow. They are familiar with water as a liquid, not in its solid form. They are also used to days and nights of equal length – very different from people who live nearer the poles, where it gets dark in the early afternoon in the winter but stays light till late evening in the summertime.

In Antarctica it is always winter. When it is summer in the Southern Hemisphere, although there are three months of constant daylight at the South Pole, it is still extremely cold in the Antarctic. Only in a few sheltered places does the ice ever melt, but it is still too cold for flowers to grow and insects to hatch. In places the ice is more than 4,000 m (13,000 ft) thick.

Winter in the Arctic is also severe, but this region has a brief summer.

In the temperate zones (the regions between the tropics and the poles) the seasons progress in a never-ending cycle – spring, summer, autumn and winter. While temperate countries of the Northern Hemisphere are experiencing winter, temperate lands of the Southern Hemisphere are enjoying summer. When the Southern Hemisphere moves into winter, it is time for the Northern Hemisphere to have summer. This is shown below:

Water has frozen into ice around these rosehips.

Northern Hemisphere			
Winter	Spring	Summer	Autumn
December	March	June	September
January	April	July	October
February	May	August	November
Summer	Autumn	Winter	Spring
Southern Hemisphere			

A beautiful sunset adds color to this bare, wintry landscape.

Why seasons happen

To understand why seasons happen we need to know a little about the movement of the earth in space. Days and nights occur because our planet spins on its axis, which is marked by the North and South Poles. Each spin takes twenty-four hours. When one side of the earth is facing the sun, that part is in daylight. When the same side moves into darkness it is nighttime. In the tropics, which are the middle zone extending for 2,400 km (1,490 mi) on either side of the equator, day and night are of equal length (twelve hours) and temperatures stay almost the same throughout the year.

In the temperate and polar zones, however, the length of days and nights varies considerably. At the extremes, which means the poles, the days are twenty-four hours long for three months in summer and the nights are twenty-four hours long for three

The Inuit build solid snow igloos to protect them from the Arctic winter.

months in winter. So the poles have three months of constant daylight and three months of darkness. This is due to the fact that the earth is tilted as it travels for 365¼ days around the sun. It is tilted at an angle of 23½°.

On March 21, the sun is directly overhead at the equator, and days and nights everywhere are of equal length. This is known as an equinox. For the next three months the northern part of the earth is tilted toward the sun. Days in the Northern Hemisphere become longer and warmer until summer reaches right into the Arctic. While it is summer in the north, winter is happening in the south.

On June 21, the sun is directly above the Tropic of Cancer. On this date it is midwinter in the Southern Hemisphere and midsummer in the Northern Hemisphere.

Then the earth starts to tilt the other way, and it is the turn of the Southern Hemisphere to move toward summer and the Northern Hemisphere to have winter. By September 23, the sun is back over the equator and the second equinox occurs, when day and night are of equal length everywhere.

In Australia, New Zealand, South Africa and the southern parts of South America, spring and summer occur when the Tropic of Capricorn is closest to the sun. By December 21, which is midsummer in the south, it is midwinter in the Northern Hemisphere.

Diagram 1 *shows how the tilt of the earth changes during the year, as the earth moves around the sun. This affects the amount of sunlight and heat that reach different parts of the earth, which causes the seasons to change.*

Diagram 2 *shows what happens on December 21, when the sun is over the Tropic of Capricorn. Because the earth is curved, the sun's rays travel through less atmosphere to reach the Southern Hemisphere and so are concentrated. However, they must pass through more atmosphere to reach the Northern Hemisphere and so are much weaker there.*

Diagram 3 *shows what happens on June 21, when the sun is over the Tropic of Cancer. Now the sun's rays are stronger in the Northern Hemisphere, where it is midsummer, and weaker in the Southern Hemisphere, where it is midwinter.*

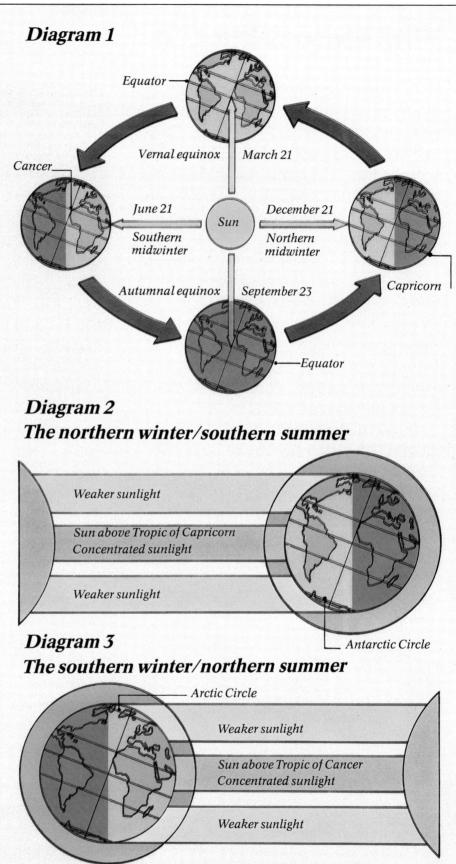

Diagram 1

Equator

Vernal equinox — March 21

Cancer

June 21
Southern midwinter

Sun

December 21
Northern midwinter

Autumnal equinox — September 23

Capricorn

Equator

Diagram 2
The northern winter/southern summer

Weaker sunlight

Sun above Tropic of Capricorn
Concentrated sunlight

Weaker sunlight

Antarctic Circle

Diagram 3
The southern winter/northern summer

Arctic Circle

Weaker sunlight

Sun above Tropic of Cancer
Concentrated sunlight

Weaker sunlight

Winter weather

In the northern temperate zone the months December, January and February are generally considered to be the winter months. In this zone, the shortest day of the year is December 21, although it comes quite near the beginning of winter, and not in the middle.

The reason why the shortest day is so near the beginning of winter is quite complex. As the earth's Southern Hemisphere tilts toward the sun, the Northern Hemisphere moves away from it. Days become shorter in the Northern Hemisphere, until the winter solstice, the shortest day, occurs on December 21. However, the air and oceans still retain heat from the summer sun. While the days are growing shorter, the air and oceans are very gradually cooling down. When they have cooled completely, the cold winter weather begins. The coldest weather usually occurs in February, long after the shortest day has passed.

In the Southern Hemisphere the seasons are reversed. June, July and August are the winter months, with August often being the coldest month. As in the Northern Hemisphere, the coldest weather occurs after the shortest day, June 21.

When we think of cold weather, snow comes to mind. Snow first forms as tiny ice crystals in the high clouds at temperatures of −20°C to −40°C (−4°F to −40°F). The crystals melt, freeze again and then join up with

Snow crystals under a microscope.

other crystals, forming snowflakes. When the snowflakes land on the ground, they soon melt, but if they freeze again, they form a layer of ice.

When cold winter winds blow, the temperature falls to many degrees below zero. Snow can then be very useful, acting like a blanket that keeps the soil beneath it warmer than the icy air above. A layer of snow protects plants and animals from icy winds.

Snow falls heavily in Canada, Scandinavia, the central U.S., Siberia and in mountainous regions, such as the European Alps and Scotland. Frost often occurs in winter and sometimes pellets of ice fall, known as hail. On some winter mornings and evenings fog or mist envelops the landscape, creating a hazy effect.

Some cross-country skiers enjoying deep snow in Washington State.

Winter around the world

While winter in the Arctic and Antarctic is a season of continuous frost and darkness, winter in the temperate zones is less harsh. Sometimes icy winds blow straight from the poles and keep everything frozen solid. At other times warmer winds from the tropics penetrate long distances into those countries that are having winter.

One temperate region, which is sometimes called "the gulf of winter warmth," is northwestern Europe. Owing to the spinning of the earth, the normal direction of prevailing winds in the temperate zones is from west to east. In the North Atlantic the wind direction is influenced by a great ocean current called the Gulf Stream. This brings warm water from the Gulf of Mexico northeastward along the coast and from there across the Atlantic Ocean to Europe. Passing around the British Isles, it continues northward and enters the Arctic Circle, keeping the coast of Norway free from ice. By constrast, the Gulf of St. Lawrence in Canada is covered with thick ice, although it lies 2,400 km (1,490 mi) south of Norway.

A frosty winter's day in Cologne, West Germany, but the wide Rhine River has not frozen over.

The Arizona Desert usually has a hot, subtropical climate. In very harsh winters, however, snow sometimes falls there, as this photograph proves.

Mountain villages in the Swiss Alps often have deep snow in winter. This is because at high altitudes the temperature is often cold enough for snow.

In the temperate zones, westward-facing coasts have lots of rain and snow in winter, but less hard frost than occurs in the middle of continents. In particular, Europe in winter is a constant battleground between mild Atlantic air and cold Siberian air, with sometimes one and sometimes the other winning. The interiors of Canada, the U.S. and Russia are entirely exposed to Arctic air currents streaming down from the North Pole. This is because there are no mountain barriers along the Arctic shores to stop the cold air currents.

In the United States the Mississippi valley gives a clear passage to warm air moving north from the Gulf of Mexico, but when it meets cold currents from the Arctic, it causes violent blizzards. Similarly there are no barriers of high land in the Southern Hemisphere to stop currents of polar air sweeping up from the Antarctic. In the southern winter such currents often bring severe weather to Australia, South Africa and Patagonia in South America. In Africa, Antarctic frosts have been known to affect tropical vegetation as far north as Zambia.

How animals escape winter

When faced with an icy winter, animals and birds have two obvious alternatives – either to adapt themselves to survive the hard times ahead or to try to escape. Many birds, being able to fly, choose the second alternative. Therefore, each autumn in the Northern Hemisphere vast numbers of birds migrate from the Arctic toward the tropics. In colder parts of the Southern Hemisphere, such as southern Australia, New Zealand and Patagonia in South America, birds fly northward to the tropics to escape winter.

Some go farther than others. Many of the geese, ducks and wading birds that nest on the shores of the Arctic Ocean in Europe and Asia tend to move southwestward, rather than due south. They are content to go no farther than western Europe, where the winters are fairly mild and they can find food. Similar species from the Canadian Arctic tend to travel much farther south. And swallows that have nested in Europe during the summer journey right across the tropics to South Africa, where the weather is milder, since it is summer there.

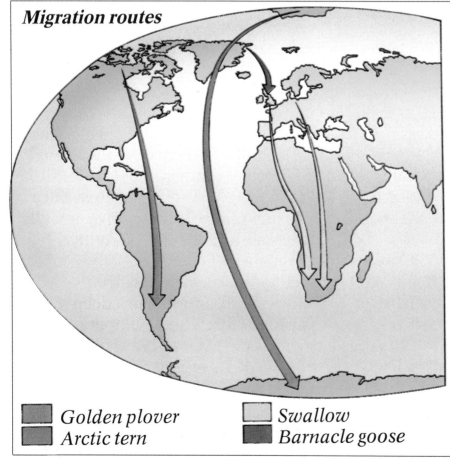

Migration routes

Golden plover
Arctic tern
Swallow
Barnacle goose

Migration
Each autumn millions of birds leave the country where they were born or bred their young. They fly to countries having warmer weather and stay there until autumn. Then it is time to return to their breeding ground, where spring has returned. The map (left) shows the migration routes of four long-distance fliers. The Arctic tern flies farthest, traveling over 17,000 km (10,500 mi) south from the Arctic to the Antarctic.

This brimstone butterfly is spending the winter in hibernation. Brimstones can be seen on the wing in Europe on mild late winter days.

Three garden dormice (Old World rodents) hibernating in their nest of nuts and leaves. They are huddled together to keep as warm as possible.

Some animals, too, migrate to avoid the worst of the winter weather. Caribou trek south in immense herds from the treeless tundra to the taiga – the cold coniferous forests of North America and Eurasia. Here they spend the winter.

A large number of animals, however, are not equipped to make long journeys and so have to stay where they are. Many of them choose to hibernate. In autumn they fatten up on the abundant food and then find a suitable secret place for their winter sleep. Bears (except for polar bears) hibernate in caves; some small rodents sleep in nests of grass and leaves.

Beavers do not hibernate, but protect themselves for the winter in island lodges accessible only through underwater tunnels. Most butterflies cannot survive winter weather, but a few, including the brimstone, actually hibernate and awaken as soon as warmer weather arrives.

Hibernation has its dangers, however. It is more than a deep sleep. The dormouse's body temperature falls so low that it feels as cold as if it were dead. Its muscles are stiff, its heartbeat is extremely faint, and it seems not to be breathing. So it is in no condition to wake up and run away if a predatory animal happens to find it.

How animals adapt to winter

Some animals that remain active throughout the winter adapt themselves to the harsh conditions by growing white coats. Examples are stoats, Arctic hares and Arctic foxes. The color change occurs in response to falling temperatures and is sometimes quite sudden. Certain birds, too, change into white plumage for winter, so that predators will find it harder to see them against a snowy background. The ptarmigan, which is a kind of grouse, roosts in tunnels which it makes in the snow.

A strange process known as delayed implantation enables the young of certain animals to bypass winter. What happens is that, after such animals have mated, the fertilized eggs remain floating in the female's uterus for several months. Then, when the time is right, the eggs attach themselves to the walls of the uterus and start to grow.

Roe deer, Old World deer of the Northern Hemisphere, are an example of a species in which delayed implantation occurs. These deer mate in July and August, and, as their

An Arctic fox in its white winter coat blends in with the snow.

gestation period is five or six months, the young would normally be born in the coldest part of the northern winter. Fortunately, delayed implantation ensures that the fertilized eggs do not start to develop until December. So the fawns (as the young deer are called) are born in May or June, which is summer in the Northern Hemisphere, when there is plenty of food and they have the best possible chance of survival. Other animals that employ delayed implantation are stoats, martens and badgers.

Most insects, including butterflies, spend the winter in either the egg or the pupa stages, in which they are immune to frost. In fact some pupae will develop properly only if they are frozen for a period. There are insects, however, that can survive as caterpillars or larvae. In the temperate zones there are sufficient numbers of insects' eggs and pupae to provide food for insect-eating birds and animals all the winter, but plenty always survive to produce new generations when summer comes.

The illustration below shows how animals' coats change color in winter.

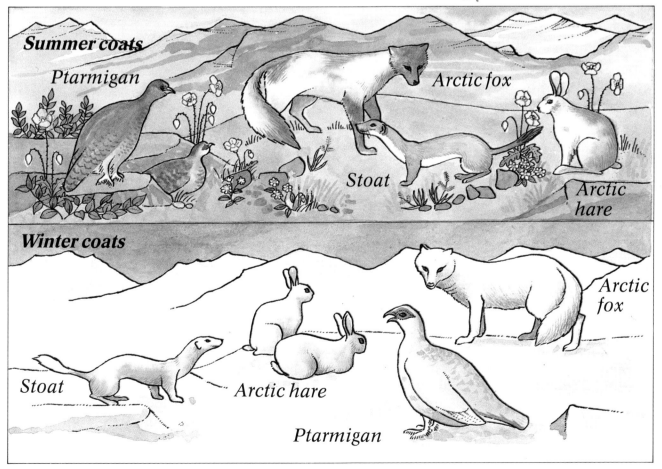

Flowers and trees in winter

Unlike animals and birds, plants have to stay where they are and make the best of winter conditions. In the seed stage, however, they are virtually immune to any sort of weather, for seeds can be frozen for months without coming to any harm. Some of them are protected by the flesh of berries or fruits which, during the course of the winter, are eaten by birds or animals. The seeds are then dropped to fall on the ground where, with luck, they will be buried by dead leaves and will start to grow in spring.

Small perennial plants, such as daisies, thistles and many grasses, rely for survival on deep root systems. The only part of them visible above ground is a rosette of leaves, lying flat on the surface and walked on by passing animals and humans. But deep in the soil, below the reach of frost, the roots are still alive and healthy.

Deciduous trees are those that shed their leaves in autumn. They are really using the same technique as the grasses; that is, they withdraw all their strength from the parts above ground and concentrate on the survival of the roots. In effect, both deciduous trees and small perennial plants are like hibernating animals. They are going to sleep through the winter.

Evergreen trees and bushes behave rather differently. They retain their leaves all through the winter, though they do shed them at intervals in other seasons. The leaves come to no harm

through being frozen, but evergreen plants use special methods to avoid being damaged by the weight of snow clinging to their foliage. Evergreen leaves are hard and fibrous, with glossy surfaces that help the snow to slide off them. Their shapes also make it hard for snow to stick. Some have a series of well-designed curves, while the leaves of pines and firs are so thin and slender that they are called needles. The larch tree has needle-shaped leaves, but it sheds them every autumn and grows new ones in spring. So it is not an evergreen.

Above *A gorse bush blooming next to a tree with willow catkins.*

Left *A wintry scene of bare deciduous trees and an evergreen in leaf.*

Below *The cheerful yellow flowers of winter aconite blooming in snow.*

Although no plants bloom in polar regions in winter, some are able to do so in temperate regions. They include garden flowers like snowdrops, aconites, Christmas roses and a few early crocuses. Their petals look delicate but are not damaged by quite severe frosts. Some shrubs flower in late winter, such as daphne mezereum, wintersweet, witch hazel and yellow jasmine. The prickly wild bush, gorse, blooms throughout the year, producing a few flowers in winter. In late winter various trees, such as birch and willow, produce catkins.

Winter on the farm – crops

Some people might suppose that the best regions of the earth for farming were the tropics, especially those areas that have enough rain to keep plants growing all the time. In such warm, moist climates farmers can gather three, four or even more crops per year from the same field. Yet vast amounts of grain are produced in the temperate zones – and that is partly because they have a winter!

The problem with growing crops continuously in the tropics is that it gives the soil no time to rest and recover. Also the heavy rains, which make it possible to grow several crops each year, wash away the soil nutrients on which the plants feed.

In temperate zones, farmers have to work hard through the other seasons to sow, grow and harvest their crops of food plants. When in autumn they finish the harvest, they plow the land ready for next year's crops. Plowing buries all the stubble, weeds and other dead plant matter deep in the soil. During the winter, bacteria and other microorganisms in the soil recycle the dead plant matter. They extract the plant foods and return them to the soil, ready for the next crop.

Hard frosts in winter make the farmer's work much easier. For sowing he likes to have a fine, crumbly soil, which makes a good seedbed. If in autumn he plows the soil and leaves it in rough, hefty clods, the winter weather does most of the work for

Fruit farmers prune their trees in late winter to remove dead branches and encourage new, healthy growth.

him. It freezes the water in the soil, so causing the clods to break up when the thaw comes. All the farmer then has to do is to level the soil with harrows. In the tropics, where no frost occurs, farmers have the hard task of breaking up the clods with hoes and mattocks.

Farmers in temperate regions now have a new range of crop varieties, especially types of wheat and barley, which are sown in autumn and are hardy enough to survive most winters. They send down deep roots below the frost level and are able to make rapid growth when spring comes. Even so, farmers allow most fields to have a good winter's rest with frost treatment, from time to time.

On the island of Oland in southern Sweden, the climate is mild enough for farmers to plant lettuce seedlings in late winter.

An English field lies fallow in winter. Snow and frost make the soil crumbly, which leaves less work for the farmer.

Winter on the farm – animals

A British farm proverb says that a farmer spends five months of the year gathering enough food to feed his farm animals for the other seven months. That is reasonably accurate for Britain, though many countries in the temperate regions have longer summers and shorter winters. In the days before there were canned and frozen foods it was true for human beings as well – the harvest of one year had to keep them supplied with food until the next harvest was ready.

Most farm animals are herbivorous, meaning that they live on food taken from plants. Therefore many of the crops the farmer grows are intended for feeding to his animals. Cattle, sheep, goats and horses all eat grass. Some of it they eat in summer, when it is growing, and some has to be conserved for winter food. The grass can be kept as hay or as silage – compressed grass. Other crops, such as kale and turnips, are grown as extra animal food, as they can stand certain degrees of frost.

During the winter months the farmer feeds cereals to all his livestock, including pigs and poultry, as well as those already mentioned. Such cereals are meal and specially prepared mixtures made from wheat, barley, oats and feed corn. If he has not grown enough crops of his own, the farmer buys supplies from dealers.

With their woolly fleeces, sheep can survive in very cold weather. The sheep pictured here are on the Canterbury Plains in New Zealand.

During cold weather most chickens are kept in a barn or hut.

The other basic need for farm livestock in winter is shelter. Pigs need the warmest quarters, because their skin has only a thin covering of bristles. Young cattle and beef cattle will live outdoors if they are given a certain amount of shelter from cold winds, such as a hedge, a wood or a simple shed, but dairy cows and calves need a comfortable building, as do horses. Poultry are now normally kept in temperature-controlled buildings or in a warm barn. Free-range poultry should at least be kept indoors in bad winter weather.

Sheep are the farm animals best suited to outdoor life in winter. They are naturally mountain animals and are not much worried by frost and cold winds, if they are well fed. If they are expected to lamb in winter, however, then they need to be brought indoors. Even sheep that are used to living outdoors sometimes have to be brought into buildings when blizzards are forecast.

Christian and Pre-Christian winter festivals

In the Northern Hemisphere the great winter festival is Christmas, which Christians celebrate as Christ's birthday. Whether Jesus was really born on December 25, no one knows, but Christians have long thought it fitting to hold the festival in midwinter. They point out that when the world was at its darkest, Jesus Christ came to bring light.

When Christians sing the carol "Good King Wenceslas," they refer to "the Feast of Stephen." St. Stephen's feast day falls on December 26, now better known as "Boxing Day." The original "boxes" were earthenware "piggy-banks" presented to servants and children on this day for storing their pennies.

The Feast of Epiphany is another traditional Christmas festival, which occurs on January 6. Epiphany is a Greek word meaning "manifestation" and the feast celebrates the presentation of the baby Jesus to the three wise men, who then offered their gifts of gold, frankincense and myrrh.

Festivals celebrating the winter solstice, or shortest day (which can be either December 21 or 22) were held

Dazzling Christmas decorations at the Rockefeller Center in New York.

long before the arrival of Christianity and many Christmas customs began in those days. The Vikings kept the Feast of Yule at midwinter. Like the Anglo-Saxons, they had a god named Odin or Woden, who was able to fly through the air on horseback. Through the long centuries since that time, Woden has become Father Christmas, or Santa Claus, while his horse has been changed into a team of reindeer.

Around midwinter the Romans celebrated the Feast of Saturnalia, which lasted fourteen days from December 17 to the start of the New Year. A feature of this feast was the giving of gifts to friends and relations.

In Sweden, where the winter solstice festival begins early (on December 13), it is traditional for villagers to choose a "Lucia Queen." She must belong to the village and be the youngest girl in a family. One duty she must perform is to bring her parents breakfast in bed. Not many years ago the Lucia Queen used to ride pillion on horseback through the streets, accompanied by maids of honor and boy attendants, to celebrate the conquest of winter by the sun.

A proud moment for the newly chosen Lucia Queen of a Swedish village.

Jewish, Sikh and Buddhist winter festivals

The Jewish festival, *Chanukah*, has a historical background. The story is that, after defeating their enemies in a great battle more than 2,000 years ago, the Jewish soldiers returned to their temple in Jerusalem. Inside they found among the ruins a small container of oil. It was fuel for their sacred, branched candlestick on which the flame was never to go out. Although the container held only enough oil for one day, it miraculously kept the candles alight for eight days until a new supply of fuel could be obtained.

Sikh women and children celebrating the festival of Lohri.

Ever since then *Chanukah* has been celebrated as a Feast of Light. Throughout the eight days of the Feast, candles are lit in branched candlesticks called Menorahs. Menorahs, now lit by electricity, blaze from the tops of public buildings in Israel. At *Chanukah* there are special foods for children to enjoy. Just as at Christmas, Christian children eat Christmas puddings, cakes and mince pies, so Jewish children at *Chanukah* eat potato pancakes and jam-filled doughnuts.

Sikhs in India and around the world celebrate the festival of *Lohri* in their lunar month *Poh*, which corresponds to January. This feast celebrates the end of winter and is a special occasion for young women. Festivities take place at night, when huge bonfires are lit. Young women dance around the fire and sweets are eaten or thrown into the flames.

Buddhists in Japan hold a festival right at the end of winter called *Setsubon*. The purpose of the festival is to drive out all evil spirits before spring arrives. First the head of the household places a container of beans on the family shrine. As the evening comes, he removes the beans and scatters them in all the entrances of the house and in dark corners. As he does so, he shouts "Devils out! Good luck in!" Finally he places a small charm above each entrance to the house, to prevent the evil spirits from returning.

Candles of the menorah decorate Jewish homes during the Festival of Light.

Below *Chanukah celebrations at the Western Wall, Jerusalem.*

More winter festivals

During winter other very colorful celebrations occur. In the Northern Hemisphere the New Year is a winter event and is widely celebrated. On New Year's Eve it is usual for relatives and friends to hold a party. When the clock strikes midnight people join hands, sing Auld Lang Syne (a song to remember old times), and wish one another a happy New Year.

In Britain, Scottish people hold New Year celebrations called Hogmanay. There, on New Year's Eve, some people dance in traditional dress to music played on bagpipes. One Scottish New Year custom is called "first footing." The Scots believe that the first person to enter their home on New Year's Day may bring good or bad luck. A dark-haired man carrying a piece of coal for the fire is thought to bring good luck. So it has become a custom to visit friends after midnight carrying a piece of coal as a sign of good luck for the coming year.

The Chinese also hold special celebrations for their own New Year, *Yuan Tan*, which begins in winter between January 21 and February 19. Street processions are held to music, with actors dressed up as dragons (a symbol of strength and good luck) and friendly lions. Firecrackers are set off, which the Chinese believe will scare away all evil spirits at the start of the year.

During winter in the Northern Hemisphere, forty days before Easter, the period of Lent begins. This is traditionally a time when Christians give up some luxury or special foods. Lent begins on Ash Wednesday and the previous day, Shrove Tuesday, is often celebrated as a feast day. This is traditionally the last day for people to eat special foods that were forbidden during Lent. It became popular to eat pancakes and this custom is still kept today on Shrove Tuesday. In parts of the United States and in Britain, pancake-eating races are held.

Musicians and street performers take part in traditional Carnival celebrations in Cologne, West Germany.

During the Chinese New Year people perform in the streets dressed as lions and dragons.

In the southern United States and in the Caribbean, Mardi Gras festivities are held from January 6 (Epiphany) to Shrove Tuesday, which is also called Mardi Gras, meaning "fat Tuesday." Carnival processions are held in the streets, and people parade to music, wearing masks and costumes. Similar carnivals before Lent are held in many European countries.

Every year in Quebec, Canada, a festival is held in the winter, when people make fabulous ice sculptures and skating events are held. Another important day in some countries is St. Valentine's Day on February 14, when it is traditional to send a secret card to a sweetheart.

Winter sports

Outdoor winter sports are, naturally, energetic. The least popular position in a game of ice hockey on a freezing winter afternoon is that of a goalie on the better team. If his team is good enough to keep the play in the opponents' half of the field, he soon feels the cold, standing alone in the goal area. Baseball, which involves most of the players standing at fixed points in the field, is no winter game.

Some sports, however, are intended for winter. Skiing, tobogganing and bobsledding depend on snow and ice.

They would be hard to practice in other seasons. Skating is popular in cold parts of the country where rivers and lakes freeze over for weeks at a time. It can, of course, be practiced on indoor rinks. Cross-country skiing is a popular sport in cold countries, and is gaining favor in the northern United States. Joggers often run in winter as well as summer. To many young people, mountaineering or rock-climbing in winter offers a tremendous challenge, though bad weather can make it very dangerous.

Playing soccer is a good way to keep warm on cold days.

In most towns and cities there are good indoor sports facilities. Many people keep fit in winter by playing indoor squash, badminton or basketball or by going swimming in indoor pools. Dance and exercise classes are also popular.

Hunting is a traditional country sport that takes place in winter. In some U.S. states and in other countries such as Britain foxhunting is popular. Foxes are chased by huntsmen on horseback, who follow a pack of foxhounds who have been trained to sniff out the fox. However, many people now protest against foxhunting because they feel it is a very cruel way to kill the fox.

Ice skating is a popular winter activity, whether on a frozen lake or ice rink.

Winter recreations

With its short, cold days, winter is the season for indoor entertainments, such as parties, plays and indoor games. Christmas and the New Year are often celebrated with parties, where traditional games may be held. Charades is a popular choice – one person mimes the title of a song, book or movie, and the others have to guess what it is. In another game the names of famous people are written on pieces of paper. Each guest has a different name pinned to his or her back without seeing the names. Then, by asking questions of the other guests, each must learn what name he or she is wearing.

During Christmas holidays in England, some children may go with their parents to the pantomime – a comic play based on a fairytale. The actors all wear bright costumes and the audience is asked to cheer the good characters and hiss at the bad ones.

A scene from a nativity play, in which schoolchildren act the story of the birth of Jesus in Bethlehem.

These people are feeding ducks on a winter's day in St. James's Park, London, England. Shown in the background is Buckingham Palace.

In countries that have plenty of snow in winter, building snowmen is a popular activity.

In the Northern Hemisphere, where Christmas occurs in winter, churches and Sunday schools often stage a nativity play. Such plays celebrate the birth of Jesus in a stable and the visit of the shepherds and wise men. In Australia, which lies in the Southern Hemisphere, nativity plays are held at the end of the summer school term.

Winter is a good time for taking up an indoor hobby, such as painting, origami (paper folding) or stamp collecting. Often it is a difficult to get outdoor exercise in winter. In countries that have a lot of snow, children build snowforts and stage snowball fights. And it is fun to build a snowman. Give the snowman a face, using carrot slices for eyes and mouth, and a whole carrot for a nose!

Winter clothes

In the tropics where there is no winter, the people rarely need heavy clothes. In the temperate and polar regions, however, where the winters can be cold and harsh, people need warm, weatherproof clothing.

As winter approaches, we are glad to put on our overcoats, scarves and gloves when we go outdoors. Among the most useful inventions of recent times are rubber boots, which enable us to splash through puddles without getting our feet wet. We ought really to take just as much trouble with the other end of the body. In science classes we learn that heat rises, and therefore, much of our body heat is lost through our heads if we do not wear hats.

We are fortunate in having new synthetic fabrics that are very efficient at keeping out the wind. Our ancestors needed several layers of heavy clothing to keep warm, but we can wear lightweight clothes that prevent our body heat from escaping, while keeping out the cold wind. Track suits are a good example, as are quilted, waterproof parkas filled with warm, light padding. Lightweight, padded ski suits are also made of this material.

Nowadays we have very good waterproof clothing. Woven fabrics can be treated with a special water-resistant finish, so that the rain runs off the fabric and does not penetrate the fibers. Plastic raincoats are probably the most waterproof of all.

Special ski suits are lightly padded and waterproof, so that they keep the wearer warm and dry.

Pullovers made of pure wool are a good idea in winter, because the wool keeps the wearer warm, just as the fleece keeps the sheep warm.

People who play football in winter only need to wear their regular uniforms. The exercise soon warms them up, but the players must take a warm shower and dress in winter clothes as soon as the game is over.

Winter illnesses can often be avoided by wearing warm, waterproof clothes, as well as eating good food and taking exercise.

We need different types of clothing for cold or wet weather.

Clothing for snow

Clothing for rain

Winter in art

Every year winter produces some dramatic and beautiful scenes which inspire artists to paint them. The painter of the medieval snowscene gives a clear idea of a heavy snowfall in a small village. Snow carpets the ground, even covering the frozen stream. It is evidently too cold for many people to be outside, as we learn from the people sitting inside the inn. The two villagers in the foreground are preparing a wild boar for a meal later on that day.

A snow-covered village in medieval times.

A fair on the frozen Thames River by Abraham Hondius.

Another picture of winter activities is "Frost fair on the Thames" by Abraham Hondius. This picture shows London in 1684 and the Thames River frozen over. The solid ice can support many stalls and crowds of people. However, the ice is melting on one part of the river and the water has been covered with a plank. Notice the fire burning in the stall on the right.

The picture of the frosty field in early winter was painted in 1873 by the French painter, Camille Pissarro. He has captured the soft light from the winter sun upon the frosted grass and crumbly earth. Notice the regular pattern of shadows that cross the field and track. These shadows are probably cast by a line of tall, narrow poplar trees just out of the picture. When you first looked at the picture, you probably did not notice the peasant carrying a bundle of sticks. This is because he is almost in the shadow, and our eyes first focus on the landscape as a whole.

Camille Pissarro painted this scene of a frosty field warmed by faint winter sun.

Winter in literature

In northern temperate countries where winters are harsh, the bleak weather is a favorite subject for writers. Shakespeare describes the essence of a cold English winter in this extract from "Love's Labours Lost":

When icicles hang by the wall,
And Dick the shepherd blows his
nail,
And Tom bears logs into the hall
And milk comes frozen home in
pail,
When blood is nipped and ways be
foul,
Then nightly sings the staring owl –
Tu-who
Tu-whit, tu-who, a merry note . . .

A leaf in winter edged with frost.

In Southern Hemisphere countries like Australia, New Zealand and South Africa, winters are less harsh. The following poem "Winter in the garden" by Dorothea MacKellar describes a mild Australian winter:

Most of the garden is asleep
Though leaves are hanging thickly
still
For night hours bring a frosty chill,
But southern slumber's never deep.

The lovely autumn's hardly gone,
Yet violets peer warily,
And roses opening charily
All frosty pink, still linger on.

. . . The snail has sealed his portal
well
With papery white; and folded up
As smooth as water in a cup
He sleeps within his stripèd shell.

. . . The garden's sleep is light and
brief
Before the subtle spring's
confessed,
Lightly it takes its hour of rest,
As lightly as unfolds the leaf.

The English proverb below links winter weather with summer:

If in February there be no rain
Tis neither good for hay nor grain
If February give much snow
A fine summer it doth foreshow.

Frost creates a magical effect on familiar objects, such as a glass windowpane.

In the Bible, the writer of the book of Job describes how winter weather is created:

He showers down snow, white as wool,
And sprinkles hoar-frost thick as ashes;
Crystals of ice he scatters like breadcrumbs;
He sends the cold, and water stands frozen
He utters his word, and the ice is melted;
He blows with his wind and the waters flow.

A row of icicles hanging by a wall inspired Shakespeare to begin the famous rhyme printed opposite.

Things to do – Looking at nature in winter

If you live in the country, look for animal tracks after an overnight fall of snow. A good guidebook will tell you what kind of animal left the tracks.

You can make a plaster cast of the animal print. You need a tube coated inside with petroleum jelly.

Place this over the print and push lightly into the soil. Pour in some plaster of Paris to cover the print. Leave for a few hours. When set, lift out the tube. Inside the set plaster should show a reverse impression of the print. Remove the plaster cast, brush it and coat with a clear varnish. Now replace the cast in the tube and pour on fresh plaster of Paris. When this has set, carefully remove the mold from the tube. You should now have an exact copy of the pawprint left by the animal in the snow.

Making a plaster footprint

You need a cardboard tube, a plastic bucket, petroleum jelly, a brush, clear varnish and some plaster of Paris, mixed quickly with water to reduce air bubbles.

1 Greasing the tube

2 Placing tube over print
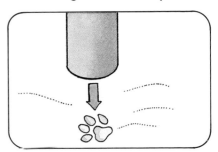

3 Adding plaster of Paris

4 Lifting out the cast
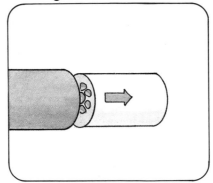

5 Brushing the cast
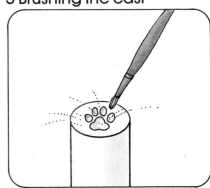

6 Varnishing the print

7 Adding fresh plaster
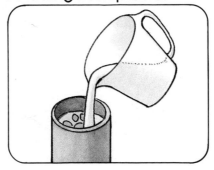

8 Removing the final cast

Clear winter nights are ideal for studying the stars. In particular, learn the positions of certain key stars and constellations, as they can help you to find your way in the dark. In the north you should be able to find the Pole Star, by using the constellation of Ursa Major (the Great Bear) as a pointer. If you live in the Southern Hemisphere you should be able to find the Southern Cross.

In winter you can find the planets Mars, Jupiter, Venus and Saturn. If you can look through some binoculars, you will be able to see some of Jupiter's moons. You may even see a man-made satellite, looking like a faint star that changes its position each night.

In the country, where there is no glare from street lighting, the stars are clearer than in towns.

Constellations in the Northern Hemisphere

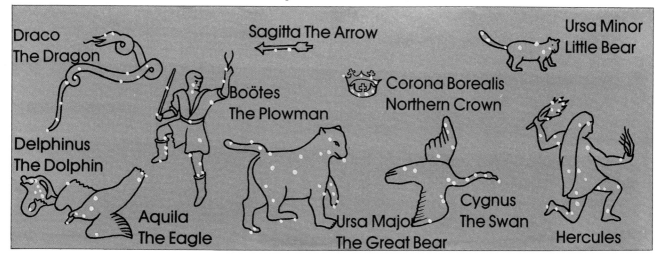

Constellations in the Southern Hemisphere

Things to do – Making winter decorations

For Christians living in the Northern Hemisphere, Christmas falls in winter. In some countries, children make candle decorations called "Christingles." To make a Christingle, stick a tall candle into an orange. Decorate the orange base with candies, nuts and ribbons. The orange represents the world and the candle stands for Christ, the light of the world.

An American custom that is spreading to many other parts of the world is to hang a decoration on the front door at Christmas. Here is how to make a door wreath from some evergreens. You need a circular frame of wire (such as a coathanger twisted into shape) or a polystyrene ring. Bind bushy evergreen branches onto the ring, using soft wire. The evergreens should completely cover the wire frame. Now tie a bow of stiff red ribbon onto the top of the wreath. Finally, tie on some small red bells or baubles and display it on your door.

A traditionally decorated Christingle

Making a door wreath

1 Making wire frame

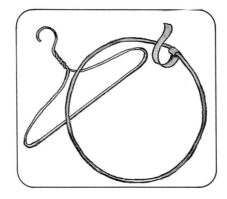

2 Binding on evergreens

3 Tying bow

4 Decorating with bells

Very few shrubs bloom in the winter, but you can make paper blossom trees to brighten your home. You will need some small bare branches from a tree and a pack of pink tissue paper.

Draw many circles of about 2½ inches or more onto the tissue paper – draw around a jam jar lid or a small glass. Cut out the circles and fold into eight. Cut scallops along the edges to make frilled petals. Open out each circle and pinch the center between your fingers, twisting it into a small stem. Bind firmly with thread. Tie the paper flowers onto the branches to look like blossoms.

Making paper blossom

1 Making circles

2 Folding into eight

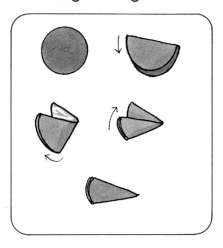

3 Scalloping edges

4 Binding base

5 Tying on flowers

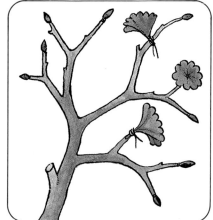

6 Displaying blossom

Things to do– Winter recipes

Some Christian groups traditionally serve pancakes on Shrove Tuesday. But they are delicious any time. This recipe is for wholewheat pancakes, but you can also make pancakes using white all-purpose flour. To make ten you need:

   ⅔ c wholewheat flour
   1¼ c milk
   1 egg
   pinch of salt
   Sift the flour and salt into a large bowl. Make a deep well in the center of the flour and put the egg inside. Add a little milk to the egg; stir in the flour from the edges. Slowly stir in the rest of the milk.

Now ask an adult to help you to cook the pancakes. First heat up oil in a non-stick frying pan and add three tablespoons of the batter, tilting the pan so the mixture spreads evenly. Cook until light brown on top and then turn the pancake over. You can use a spatula or toss it in the air. Cook the other side until brown, then turn out the pancake onto a warm plate. Make more pancakes in the same way until the batter is used up. Then add the filling.

Delicious fillings for pancakes include cooked chicken, cheese, broccoli, asparagus or ham. For sweet pancakes add lemon juice and sugar.

Making pancakes

1 Adding egg to flour

2 Stirring in milk

3 Adding batter to pan

4 Cooking the pancake

5 Tossing the pancake

6 Serving with filling

Birds get hungry in the cold winter. You can feed them with special cake.

With an adult's help melt about 4 oz of lard or suet in a saucepan. Allow it to cool and then stir in the following: 2 oz crumbs (from old bread, cake, biscuits or cornflakes), 1½ oz peanuts and some sunflower seeds.

Now take a clean, round plastic margarine container (8 oz size) and make a small hole in the center of the base. Through this thread a length of string 12 in or more. Leave a small end below the hole and tie into a knot.

Next spoon in the crumb mixture around the string and press down firmly. When the tub is full, place a saucer on the top and refrigerate overnight. To unmold the cake, turn it upside down and tap on the base. If necessary, widen the hole to allow the knot through.

Find a tree in your yard or play area and tie the cake onto a branch. After a while many birds should come to feed.

A cake decoration

Here is a simple idea to add a seasonal finish to a sponge cake. Place a paper doily on top of the cake and sift confectioner's sugar over it. Carefully remove the doily from the surface of the cake. The sugar should form a pattern like a snowflake.

Making a hanging cake

1 Adding crumbs to fat

2 Piercing the hole

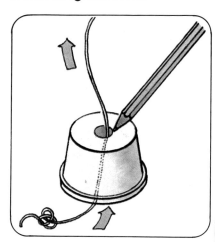

3 Unmolding the cake

4 Hanging on a tree

Glossary

Ash Wednesday   The first day of Lent.

Bacteria   Microscopic organisms, generally classified as plants.

Blizzard   Snow storm, with strong winds.

Chanukah (also written Hanukkah) Jewish festival of lights.

Christingle   A decorated orange holding a candle, symbolizing Christ, the light of the world.

Constellation   A group of stars.

Deciduous Trees   A tree that sheds its leaves annually as winter comes.

Delayed implantation   A natural process in some mammals, which delays for weeks or months the development of the egg in the female's body after it is fertilized.

Doily   A lacy decorative mat which is placed on serving plates to make cakes look more attractive.

Equator   An imaginary line around the center of the earth, located midway between the North and South Poles.

Equinox   A day that occurs twice a year, when day and night are the same length.

Fasting   Going without food, often for religious purposes.

Fertilization   The joining of a male's sperm and a female's egg.

Foliage   The leaves of a plant or tree.

Free-range   A word describing poultry that are allowed to roam freely outside.

Gestation   The period during which a young animal is growing inside the body of its mother.

Gulf Stream   The warm oceanic current that flows from the Gulf of Mexico to Europe.

Harrows   Tools to level the ground and remove weeds.

Herbivorous   Feeding on plants.

Hibernation   The process in which animals spend the winter asleep.

Immune   Resistant to a disease.

To Lamb   A term used only for ewes, meaning to give birth to a lamb.

Lent   A period of forty days between Ash Wednesday and Easter, which was traditionally a period of fasting and going without luxuries.

Mattocks   Pick-shaped tools used to break up hard ground.

Medieval   Of the Middle Ages.

Microorganism   A living creature invisible to the naked eye.

Migration   The seasonal movement of creatures from one place to another.

Nativity play   A play about the birth of Jesus Christ.

Northern Hemisphere   The northern half of the world above the equator.

Nutrients   Foods, particularly for plants.

Pantomime   A Christmas entertainment usually based on a fairy tale.

Perennial plants   Plants that continue their growth for several years.

Pillion   A cushion or seat attached behind a saddle for a second rider, usually a woman.

Plumage   A bird's set of feathers.

Predators   Creatures that prey on other creatures.

Ptarmigan   A bird of the grouse family, found in the Arctic and on high mountains.

Pupa   An insect in the third stage of its

development, between the larva and the adult insect.

Recycle   To convert waste to usable material.

Saturnalia   An ancient Roman festival of midwinter, from which some Christmas customs are derived.

Satellite   A man-made device that orbits the earth or another planet.

Shrine   Sacred tomb or altar.

Shrove Tuesday   The day before Ash Wednesday commonly known as Pancake Day.

Southern Hemisphere   The southern half of the world below the equator.

Stalking   Approaching game cautiously under cover.

Taiga   Coniferous forest on the edge of the Arctic tundra.

Temperate zones   The parts of the earth that lie between the Arctic Circle and the Tropic of Cancer, and between the Antarctic Circle and the Tropic of Capricorn.

Tropical zone   The part of the earth that lies between the tropics of Cancer and Capricorn.

Tundra   A treeless region in the Arctic, with a frozen subsoil.

Uterus   Another word for womb, the part of the female mammal in which the young animal develops before it is born.

Yule   An old term for Christmas.

Further reading

Baldwin, Barbara. **Celebrate the Seasons**. Monkey Sisters, 1983.

Bauman, Toni and June Zinkgraf. **Winter Wonders**. Good Apple, 1978.

Casey, Patricia. **Winter Days**. Putnam Publishing Group, 1984.

Cosgrove, Margaret. **It's Snowing!** Dodd, 1980.

Marcus, Elizabeth. **Our Wonderful Seasons.** Troll Associates, 1983.

Markle, Sandra. **Exploring Winter** Atheneum, 1984.

Williams, Terry T. and Ted Major. **The Secret Language of Snow.** Pantheon, 1984.

Index

Aconites 17
Africa 11
Air, cooling of 8
Anglo-Saxons 23
Animals
 farm 20–21
 wild 8, 12–13, 14–15,
  38
Antarctica 4, 10, 11
Arctic 4, 10, 11, 12
Arctic Circle 10
Arctic foxes 14
Arctic hares 14
Art 34–5
Ash Wednesday 26
Atlantic Ocean 10
Australia 7, 11, 31, 36
Autumn 4, 12, 13, 16, 18

Badgers 15
Badminton 29
Barley 20
Basketball 29
Bears 13
Beavers 13
Berries 16
Bible 37
Birds 12, 14, 38
Blizzards 11, 21
Bobsledding 28
Boxing Day 22
Brimstone butterfly 13
Britain 10, 20
Buddhist festivals 25
Butterflies 13, 15

Canada 8, 10, 11, 12, 27,
 28

Caribbean 27
Caribou 13
Carnivals 27
Caterpillars 15
Catkins 17
Cattle 20–21
Chanukah 24
Charades 30
Chinese New Year 26
Christian festivals 22
Christingles 40
Christmas 22, 30–31, 40
Christmas roses 17
Clothes 4, 32–3
Corn 20
Constellations 39
Crocuses 17
Crops 18, 20
Cross-country skiing 28

Daphne mezereum 17
Darkness 6, 10
Day, length of 8
Daylight 4, 6–7
Deciduous trees 16
Decorations 40–41
Delayed implantation 14
Dormice 13
Ducks 12

Earth
 movement around
  sun 6–8
  daily rotation of 6, 10
Easter 26
Epiphany 22, 27
Equator 6
Equinox 6

Eurasia 13
Europe 10–11, 12
European Alps 8
Evergreen trees 16

Farming 18
Father Christmas 23
Feast of Light 24
Festivals 22–27
First-footing 26
Flowers 4, 17
Fog 8
Football 28, 32
Foxhunting 29
Foxhounds 29
Frost 4, 8, 10, 11, 16, 17,
 18, 20, 21, 35

Geese 12
Goats 20
Gorse 17
Grass 20
Gulf of Mexico 10, 11
Gulf of St. Lawrence 10
Gulf Stream 10

Hail 8
Harvest 18, 20
Hay 20
Hibernation 13, 38
Hogmanay 26
Hondius, Abraham 34
Horses 20–21
Hunting 29

Ice 4, 8, 10, 28, 35, 37
Icicles 36
Indoor entertainments 30

Indoor hobbies   31
Insects   4, 15, 38

Japan   25
Jasmine   17
Jerusalem   24
Jewish festivals   24
Jogging   28
Jupiter   39

Kale   20

Leaves   16
Lent   26
Literature   36–7
Lohri   25
London   34
Lucia Queen   23

MacKellar, Dorothea   36
Mardi Gras   27
Mars   39
Martens   15
Midsummer   7
Midwinter   7, 22
Migration   12, 38
Mississippi Valley   11
Mist   8
Mountaineering   28

Nativity plays   31
New Year   23, 26, 30
New Year's Day   26
New Year's Eve   26
New Zealand   7, 36
Nighttime   6
North Pole   11
Northern Hemisphere

6, 7, 8, 12, 14, 15, 22, 26, 31, 40
Norway   10

Oats   20
Oceans, cooling of   8
Odin   23
Origami   31

Pancake Day   27
Pancake races   27
Pancakes, making   42
Pantomime   30
Patagonia   11, 12
Pigs   20–21
Pissarro, Camille   35
Plants   8, 16–17
    perennial   17
Plowing   18
Polar regions   6, 17, 32
Pole Star   39
Poles, the   4, 7, 10
Poultry   20–21
Predators   13, 14
Ptarmigan   14
Pupae   15

Quebec festival   27

Rain   8, 11, 18, 32, 37
Recipes   42–3
Rock climbing   28
Roe deer   14
Romans   23
Rosetti, Christina   37
Russia   11

Santa Claus   23

Saturn   39
Saturnalia   23
Scandinavia   8
Scotland   8
Seasons
    cycles of   4, 8
    variations   6, 8
Seeds   16
Setsubon   25
Shakespeare, William   36
Sheep   20, 21
Shrove Tuesday   26–7, 42
Shrubs   17
Siberia   8
Sikh festivals   25
Silage   20
Skating   28
Skiing   28
Snow   4, 8, 14, 28, 31, 34, 36–7, 38
Snowdrops   17
Snowman   31
South Africa   7, 11, 12, 36
South Pole   4
Southern Hemisphere   4, 7, 8, 11, 12, 31, 36
Sports
    indoor   29
    outdoor   28
Squash   29
St. Stephen's Day   22
St. Valentine's Day   27
Stamp collecting   31
Stars, observing   39
Summer   4
Swallows   12
Sweden   23
Swimming   29

Taiga   13
Temperate regions   4, 6, 8, 10–11, 15, 17, 18, 20, 32, 36
Temperature, changes in   4, 6
Thames River   35
Toboganning 28
Tracks, animal   38
Trees   16–17
Tropic of Cancer   4, 7

Tropic of Capricorn   4, 7
Tropical regions   4, 6, 10, 12, 18, 32
Tundra   13

Venus   39
Vikings   23

Water   4
Weather   8, 36, 39
Wheat   21

Winds   8, 10, 21, 32, 37
Winter solstice   22
Wintersweet   17
Witch hazel   17
Woden   23
Wolves   13

Yuan Tan   26
Yule, feast of   23

Zambia   11

Picture acknowledgments

The publishers would like to thank the following for allowing their photographs to be reproduced in this book: Bridgeman Art Library 35; Bruce Coleman Limited by the following photographers: Bryan and Cherry Alexander (7), Keith Gunner (9), D and J Bartlett (11 left), Hans Reinhard (13 right and 21), Frieder Sauer (13 left), James Simon (14), Jane Burton (17 below), Eric Crichton (17 above right), G Hunter (20), Kim Taylor (37 above), 31; Cotswold Camera (36); E.T. Archive (34 below), Geoscience Features Picture Library (19 below, 37 below); ICOREC (24 and 30), ZEFA by the following photographers: G Mabbs (4), Adam (5), F Sauer (8), Damm (10), F Villiger (11 right), John Flowerdew (16 main picture), J Pfaff (26), R Theissen (28), P. Friese (29), and also 22, 26, 31 below and 32. The remaining photographs belong to the Wayland Picture Library. All the illustrations are by Hayward Art Group.